CW00665405

just
grace

4

CONTENTS

Good news for you   6-16

Response to God   17-21

Assurance of eternal life 24

Commitment to God   25

Equipped for growth   26-32

In an uncertain world the one thing we can be sure of is that we are all going to die. But what lies beyond? Most people would like to be sure about heaven (eternal life).

Some people hope to get to heaven by being religious. Others try not to think about it. Many hope the good in their lives will outweigh the bad.

Whatever we may hope or think, the main message of the Bible is that we can be certain of eternal life – that is, life lived to the full now, and heaven when we die!

Here is what God says – from the Bible...

6

HEAVEN IS
A FREE GIFT!

"The GIFT of God is eternal
life in Christ Jesus our Lord." Romans 6:23

"By grace (God's kindness) you have
been saved, through faith – and this
is not from yourselves. It is the gift
of God." Ephesians 2:8

7

Because eternal life is a gift,
like any genuine gift...

WE CANNOT EARN IT OR DESERVE IT

The Bible says that no amount of personal effort, doing good things, or even being religious, can earn eternal life.

"It is the gift of God – NOT BY WORKS, so that no-one can boast." Ephesians 2:8-9

If God did not offer each of us a place in Heaven as a gift, no-one would get there, because...

EVERYONE HAS SINNED

To some people sin means murder, rape or armed robbery, to others it can include things like cheating on a partner. We all have our own ideas and standards - but when it comes to heaven, only God's standard is relevant.

To God, **hate and lust** are sins just as much as murder or adultery, because both express selfishness and ignorance of His Law.

God's standard doesn't stop at bad deeds or wrong thoughts.

The greatest commandments are **to love God with all our heart, soul, mind and strength, and to care for others as much as we care for ourselves.** So even apart from the bad things we may **do** or **think,** we are sinning when we do not love God or help others in need!

This is why the Bible says:

ALL HAVE SINNED and fall short of the glory of God. Romans 3:23

And because of this...

WE CAN DO NOTHING TO SAVE OURSELVES

The reason we cannot do anything to save ourselves is because we have already failed to meet God's standard of absolute perfection.

"Be perfect, therefore as your heavenly Father is perfect." Matthew 5:48

No matter how good we are, **any sin** - no matter how trivial it may appear to us - spoils the perfection that God requires.

"Whoever keeps the whole law and yet stumbles at just one point is guilty of breaking all of it. James 2:10

Whilst some people are better than others, being better is not good enough if we fall short. Imagine you had to jump across a deep chasm and fall short by just a couple of feet, are you better off than someone who only gets half way?

Because we fall short of God's standard, we are sinners, unable to save ourselves. Although we can't earn it, and we don't deserve it - God offers us eternal life as a free gift!

Why should God offer anyone the gift of eternal life?
The answer is:

GOD IS LOVING AND MERCIFUL AND DOESN'T WANT TO PUNISH US

The Bible tells us that:

"the Lord is good and **His love endures forever**" Psalm 100:5

"the Lord your God... is gracious and compassionate slow to anger and **abounding in love**" Joel 2:13

In fact the Bible says that:

"God is love" 1 John 4:8

However, His love does not overrule His justice- and the same Bible that tells us of His love also makes it abundantly clear that

GOD IS PERFECTLY JUST SO HE MUST PUNISH SIN

"All His ways are just" Deuteronomy 32:4 and God says:

"I will not acquit the guilty." Exodus 23:7

"I will punish the world for its evil, the wicked for their sins." Isaiah 13:11

"man is destined to die once, and after that to face JUDGEMENT." Hebrews 9:27

If God were to overlook our sin because of His love, He would no longer be just. His law is perfect and His sentence has been passed...

"The wages of sin is death" Romans 6:23

But, God has brought His love and His justice together in the most incredible way – in the person of Jesus Christ.

ut who is Jesus?

The Bible makes it clear that...

JESUS IS GOD

"In the beginning was the Word (Jesus), and the Word (Jesus) was with God, and the Word (Jesus) was God...The Word (Jesus) became flesh and made His dwelling among us."
John 1:1 & 14

God became a man in Jesus Christ and this is what we celebrate at Christmas.

"The virgin will be with child and will give birth to a Son, and they will call Him Immanuel – which means, **God with us.**" Matthew 1:23

But why did Jesus come into the world?

Each one of us stands condemned before God because of our sin. But because of His great love for us, He put our sins onto Jesus.

HE CAME TO PAY THE PENALTY OUR SINS DESERV

"We all, like sheep, have gone astray, each of us has turned to his own way, and the Lord has laid on [Jesus] the [sin] of us all." Isaiah 53:6

A magistrate once had a young mum in front of him who was guilty of stealing groceries from a supermarket. The magistrate knew the mother had no money to pay the fine of fifty pounds, but she could not bear to go to prison because of the distress it would cause her two children. The magistrate came down from the bench and offered to pay the fine himself. The mother accepted his kind offer and she was free! She had not earned it. She did not deserve it, but the magistrate had mercy on her. The law was upheld in that the penalty was paid in full, but at the same time love was exercised.

14

This is what God has done for us!

Jesus died on the cross to pay the penalty
for our sin and to fulfil God's justice.
On the third day He rose from the dead
and is alive forever, and He offers the gift
of eternal life to whoever will receive it.

This is what we celebrate at Easter time.

"God demonstrates His own love for us in this: While
we were still sinners, Christ died for us." Romans 5:8

The death of Jesus on the cross has repaired
our relationship with God. Now we can come
into His presence holy, pure and faultless.

15

What you have just read is the main message of the Bible; the good news of what God has done for us in Jesus. It is summed up in the following verse:

"God so loved the world that He gave His one and only Son, that WHOEVER believes in Him shall not perish but have eternal life." John 3:16

The gift of eternal life is for **WHOEVER** believes in Him and that word – whoever – includes YOU!

Do **YOU** believe in Jesus?
If you do then....

YOU CAN RECEIVE THE GIFT OF ETERNAL LIFE THROUGH FAITH

"For it is by grace you have been saved, THROUGH FAITH" Ephesians 2:8

You may have been relying on your own efforts or your human logic or even religious activity, but they cannot save you. Faith in Jesus is the only way.

But saving faith is not simply believing **about** Jesus, or reaching out to Him in a crisis – good as these things are. This saving faith requires that you...

TRANSFER YOUR TRUST TO JESUS CHRIST ALONE

When travelling to another country by aeroplane, it isn't **knowing about** the aeroplane – time, costs, routes, etc. – that gets you there. You have to act on your knowledge – exercise **FAITH** – get on the aircraft, and trust it to take you to where you want to go!

Similarly, if you **believe** what God has done for you and you want to accept His offer of eternal life, then you must act on your belief and trust Jesus Christ **alone**. There is no other way.

REPENT OF ALL YOUR SIN

"He is patient with you, not wanting anyone to perish, but everyone to come to repentance." 2 Peter 3:9

Trusting Jesus Christ alone means putting your life in His hands, acknowledging that He knows the right way for your life. This change of direction – going God's way instead of your own – is repentance.

Repentance doesn't just mean being sorry about the things you have done wrong. Of course you are sorry when you realise how much you have hurt God by going your own way – the wrong way.

Repentance is like doing a U-turn.

1 Recognise you are going the wrong way.

2 Own up to God and ask His forgiveness.

3 Start going in the opposite direction – HIS WAY.

"There is a way that seems right to a man, but in the end it leads to death." Proverbs 14:12

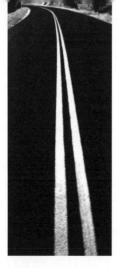

When you turn from your own way to God's way, you are acknowledging that:

JESUS IS LORD

He knows what is best for you. You can trust Him to lead you into the fulness of life so long as you do it His way. Jesus said,

"If anyone loves Me, he will obey My teaching." John 14:23

Obeying Him will mean doing some new things and also doing some things differently

Whilst you cannot be saved by doing things, living in a way that is pleasing to God will be evidence of the new life that He gives and will also confirm His Lordship in your life.

19

"We are God's workmanship, created in Christ Jesus to do good works." Ephesians 2:10

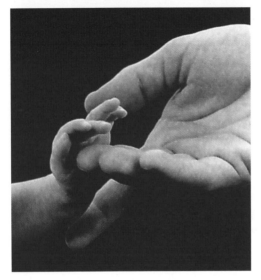

Making Jesus Lord of your life and obeying Him is not an easy option- your new life will mean some changes and certain things may be hard. God will not do the changing for you, but when you accept His gift of eternal life His Holy Spirit will live within you giving you the power to live in obedience to Him.

"He who raised Christ from the dead will also give life to your mortal bodies through His Spirit." Romans 8:11

THE SPIRIT OF GOD GIVES LIFE

God's Spirit will live within you, not only giving you a new life but at the same time giving you the power and direction for your new life.

"Flesh gives birth to flesh, but the Spirit gives birth to spirit." John 3:6

The new life that we receive through God's
Spirit means that we are part of a new family.

THE FAMILY OF GOD

"To all who received Him, to those who
believed in His name, He gave the right
to become children of God." John 1:12

"Through [Jesus] we have access to the
Father by one Spirit. Consequently we are
no longer foreigners and aliens, but fellow
citizens with God's people and members
of God's household." Ephesians 2:18-19

Children grow up best within a secure
family setting and God's children are no
exception. Belonging to the church –
which represents God's family - is as
natural for the believer as the home
is to a human family.

21

- Do you understand the good news of the Bible?
  (pages 6 to 16 of this booklet)

- Do you believe what the Bible teaches about God's gift of eternal life through Christ?

- Do you understand the response that God wants from you?
  (pages 17 to 21 of this booklet)

- Would you like to receive God's gift of eternal life?

- Will you trust Him alone for salvation?

- Do you sincerely repent of all sin and want Him to be Lord of your life?

- Would you like to become one of His children, part of His family, the church?

22

If you can say "yes" to each of these questions the prayer on the next page may help you respond to God's invitation.

Prayer of response

My Lord and my God,
I have lived my life my way.
I have done many wrong things.
I repent of all my sin.
Please forgive me.
Lord Jesus, I trust You now to be
my Saviour.
Thank You for dying in my place.
I ask You now for Your gift of
eternal life.
I give my life to You
and want You to be my Lord.
Help me to live for You
by the power of Your Holy Spirit.
These things I pray in Jesus' name.

KNOWING FOR CERTAIN

If you have truly repented (turned away) from your sins and put your trust in Jesus Christ, God wants you to **know** that you have eternal life.

The Bible says, "I write these things to you who believe in the name of the Son of God so that you may KNOW that you have eternal life." 1 John 5:13

Jesus said, "I tell you the truth, he who believes has everlasting life." John 6:47

Notice who said it – Jesus Christ!
Notice the promise applies **now**; it's not *will* have or *may* have, but **has**. Jesus says if you believe (put your trust in Him) you have eternal life. So, on the basis of what you have just prayed, read from God's word and believe in your heart, you can know that you have eternal life.

To help remind you of the decision you have made today we invite you to sign the commitment on the next page.

MY COMMITMENT TO GOD

I believe that God so loved the world that He gave His one and only Son, that whoever believes in Him will not perish but have everlasting life. I have, therefore, today, repented of all my sin and do now trust Jesus Christ to forgive me and to grant me the gift of new life – eternal life.

I resolve in the power of His Spirit to live as a member of the family of believers in obedience to Jesus as Lord. I shall seek to grow in my love toward God and in my ability to make His love known to others.

Signed
_____

Date
_____

"May the God of hope fill you with all joy and peace as you trust in Him, so you may overflow with hope by the power of the Holy Spirit." Romans 15:13

"Being confident of this, that He who began a good work in you will carry it on to completion until the day of Christ Jesus." Philippians 1:6

25

As life begins with birth, you have
been reborn by God's Spirit.
So today is the first day of the
rest of your new life – eternal life.

The surest sign of life is growth and

GOD WANTS YOU TO GROW

"Like newborn babies, crave pure spiritual milk, so that
by it you may grow up in your salvation." 1 Peter 2:2

"Grow in the grace and knowledge of our Lord Jesus Christ."
2 Peter 3 :18

God will help you grow, by:

- His living presence
- His written word
- His gift of prayer
- His loving family - the church
- His plan for your life

You will never again be alone for God the Father,
God the Son, God the Holy Spirit, has promised

HIS LIVING PRESENCE

"Do not fear for I am with you, do not be dismayed for I am
your God. I will strengthen you and help you; I will uphold you
with My righteous right hand." Isaiah 41:10

"I will be with you always," said Jesus, "to the very end of the age."
Matthew 28:20

"You yourselves are God's temple and God's Spirit lives in you."
1 Corinthians 3:16

"All scripture is God-breathed and is useful for teaching, rebuking, correcting and training in righteousness, so that the man of God may be thoroughly equipped for every good work."
2 Timothy 3:16

God wants you to know His way and His will for your life, so He has given you the Bible

HIS WRITTEN WORD

As you read and study it you will soon be saying:

"Your word is a lamp to my feet and a light for my path." Psalm 119:105

Through the Bible God speaks to you, but by prayer you speak to God.

You don't have to use any special language when you pray – just talk to Him naturally. He is much more concerned to hear from you than to be impressed, or put off, by the way you speak.

You can talk to Him at any time, anywhere, about anything by using:

HIS GIFT OF PRAYER

"Do not be anxious about anything, but in everything, by prayer and petition, with thanksgiving, present your requests to God."
Philippians 4:6

"Devote yourselves to prayer, being watchful and thankful." Colossians 4:2

29

"Until now you have not asked for anything in My name. Ask and you will receive, and your joy will be complete." John 16:24

From the birth of the church new believers were drawn to each other and together they experienced the warmth of love and acceptance as each person contributed to the spiritual well-being of others in...

HIS LOVING FAMILY
THE CHURCH

"They devoted themselves to the apostles' teaching, and to the fellowship, to the breaking of bread (communion) and to prayer." Acts 2:42

If you are in the church where God wants you to be, you will find great encouragement and strength. This will come from the services, Bible study groups and other activities, but most especially by getting to know other Christians who are spiritually mature.

God has a plan for your life which He wants you to discover.
As the Bible says...

"We are God's workmanship, created in Christ Jesus to do good works, which God prepared in advance for us to do." Ephesians 2:10

HIS PLAN FOR YOUR LIFE WILL UNFOLD AS YOU

- Enjoy His presence
- Obey His word
- Pray for His guidance
- Take your place in His family

The more you live according to His plan the more you live!

God wants you to be a faithful disciple (a follower who learns). Faithful disciples are fruitful disciples, which means they care for and tell others what they have learned so that they too can have eternal life.

"I chose you...to go and bear fruit. This is to My Father's glory, that you bear much fruit, showing yourselves to be My disciples." John 15:16 & 8

32

So, now that you have put your trust in Jesus – **tell somebody**. Make a point of telling a relative or friend within the next day or so.